Books by Leslie Adrienne Miller

Y

The Resurrection Trade
Eat Quite Everything You See
Yesterday Had a Man in It
Ungodliness
Staying Up for Love

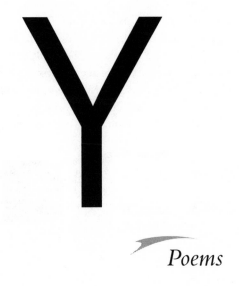

Y

Poems

Leslie Adrienne Miller

Graywolf Press

This publication is made possible in part by a grant provided by the Minnesota State Arts Board, through an appropriation by the Minnesota State Legislature from the Minnesota general fund and its arts and cultural heritage fund with money from the vote of the people of Minnesota on November 4, 2008, and a grant from the Wells Fargo Foundation Minnesota. Significant support has also been provided by the National Endowment for the Arts; Target; the McKnight Foundation; and other generous contributions from foundations, corporations, and individuals. To these organizations and individuals we offer our heartfelt thanks.

Published by Graywolf Press
250 Third Avenue North, Suite 600
Minneapolis, Minnesota 55401

www.graywolfpress.org

Published in the United States of America

ISBN 978-1-55597-622-4

2 4 6 8 9 7 5 3 1
First Graywolf Printing, 2012

Library of Congress Control Number: 2012936224

Cover design: Jeenee Lee Design

Cover art: Ron Mueck, *Boy*. Used with the permission of ARoS. Photographer: Poul Ib Henriksen.

CONTENTS

Y

Now it is each alone, and the mission becomes a race which only one may win, as, ahead of them, vast and luminous, the longed-for, the loved planet swims into view, like a moon, a sun, an image of God, round and perfect. A target.

—Margaret Atwood, "Adventure Story"

Y

Perhaps it's a thread that needs to be pulled,
a single stitch caught in the crux.

Whole word in French and Spanish,
vertical axis of Cartesian three

loaning its fragile branch to a boy
in theory. *On y va.* Let's go *There.*

What happens to unrepaired sequences
in subsequent generations? Semivowel,

blown umbrella, arrow reversed in wind,
frizzy blot of genetic code directing the symphony

of a trillion sperm, *a single Y . . . might fold over,*
line up these similar patches of genetic sequence,

and then accidentally delete everything
that lies in between. Je *est un autre.*

If the face is a christening in flesh,
the boy of him is its opposite,

raising the tent of bones in which
he will harbor all the starry anomalies

that a knowledge of God cannot undo.

THE LUCIFER EFFECT

Usually he's all noise, the hard soles
of his bare feet whapping summer-packed
earth, his signature solo of stick on fence,
table, tree, the iron chime of the hammock stand,
or the tub song through the bathroom window
ten feet from where the old lady
sleeps. But today there's the matter
of the root beer pops she keeps
at the ready, and the boy has gone
too quiet. She doesn't know which gap
in the fence his face might grace
or where a creamy arm will blast through.
He stands on the bottom rail
watching her cloudy eyes scan the slats,
wondering just how blind she is.
Learning her limits is a game he suspects
he shouldn't play, but sometimes he's quiet
on purpose: some funny place in him likes
to see her struggle to locate whatever he is
beyond squirm and din. Likes his muscles
cocked, the spring in his heart coiled
around all that could go differently.
On tiptoe, he hugs the fence, peers
at her wrinkled arm stretched toward
a long gash of sunlight between the yards.
He giggles from ten feet farther off,
so she has to turn and inch along the phlox,
arm aloft with dripping pop. He wants it, yes,
but now the mind craves more than what the tongue

already knows. Crouched in a shrub, he waits
for the moment to unfurl its enormous flock
of risks, only to wheel back and settle again.
He waits until her smile begins to slide, until
the inevitable stumble, and there it is—
tingle of dark cause, sensation ajar,
rippling along his scalp.
He's ready, now that he's made her turn
and plunge through a gush of roses,
to claim his sweet.

adversaria

> Itard was only 26 when he began the diary: "The Forbidden
> Experiment" they called it, because even then they understood
> the toxic mix of curiosity and parental vigilance, lethal as the dissolve
> between church and state. Hair retreated from the face
> so that we could read it. How much can be learned, and how much is innate?
> The question itself implies a reciprocal relationship that does not exist.

FROM A BALCONY OVER RUE DE LA HUCHETTE

It's possible to step into and out of
the shadows of walkers with the eye

alone, each block an accomplishment,
the mind's claim to more space

with less effort, unless you are
the boy inclined to experiment

with the vagaries of narrative
sequence, entirely engaged

in the problem of whether to drop
the cork in front of the woman

or on her. Looking down as a power
as long as no one below can find,

let alone open, the door he remembers
as hidden behind racks of postcards,

behind a giant spindle of lamb
shimmering in spotlit grease,

the door he remembers leads to a tiny,
slow lift and another locked door.

Therefore he decides the last drop
of wine in mother's glass might descend

differently, might be perceived
as rain, which, oddly enough, makes

anyone look up, as if a stern squint
could curb an impertinent cloud.

There was a father there too, that day,
though now that we are in their future,

a simple alteration of tense, he's not
present. We can't exactly say he's been erased.

He's simply no longer in the mind considering
the view over Rue de la Huchette,

fixing on the end of the block where
the sky arrives differently every time

she looks. What to do with the missing
agency this change in tense has caused?

Who will stop the child from flinging
the ruby lozenge of Bordeaux?

Who will stop the mother from turning
the last sip of wine into rain?

fizzee ólləjee

The man is not wholly evil—he has a Thesaurus
in his cabin.

—J. M. Barrie on Captain Hook

Why is it so amusing to know that Darwin
was obese to the degree that a half-moon
had to be cut from his dining table
to free his monstrous belly? Or that
Coleridge jumped at the chance to play
with laughing gas, while Roget,
terrified of clutter, went home to lists,
deaths and synonyms all in their place.

Better yet that Beddoes believed
in the curative powers of bovine breath
and led the nervous creatures
into hospital rooms where certainly
they filled the air with more
than the contents of their lungs.

Here is the last generation of men
schooled in flesh. Who knew
how the firm whorls of the human brain
soften too fast in a corpse, while the face
freezes hard in its final grimace.

Roget believed that words could ride
in the roomy pockets of physiology,
packed away like scales, clouds or fur,

categories, tools in a box. A list rich
in alternatives to silence. That the abstract
should commandeer the concrete, and the human
complaint of pain fall in known territory.

Alive, the human visage, is an open book,
writ with lively eyes and a ground force
of muscles that spell pleasure
or any of its prodigious antonyms.
While despots marched over maps,
the anatomists scored their paths
in flesh, promising a corpse
to every man of science,
and nervous women retired
to the seaside with trunks
of feathers and bombazine.
Until Darwin closed the garden gate,
and Adam's job was done.

HYPERPHAGIA

*The heart of another is a dark forest, always, no matter
how close it has been to one's own.*

—Willa Cather

For years I misremembered it as *The heart of another
is always a dark forest,* believing the wilderness a given,
a problem to solve *before* we're let in. That once you find
the way in, it's a wood you can know, with beasts
you can name if not outwit, even when they try
to take you by wonder. Above all, that the getting close
would unravel a path in the undergrowth, beat back
stinging snarls, so we'd arrive at some degree
of recognition, then have every reason to expect
improvement, even comfort thereafter, the screaming
and slithering thinning over the years
until it's more Hyde Park than Yellowstone.

But there's no accounting for the loneliness
of a journey we expected to share and ended up
taking solo, and though we knew there were
tunnels everywhere underfoot, that everything
living beneath the surface was as afraid of us
as we were of it, fear kept tarnishing our way,
and the grizzly of hope was always somewhere ahead
just off the path, unaccountably cute in its hunger,
swatting berries toward its giant smiling maw
as if there were years to accomplish the task
of fattening the chance of survival.

Cather knew what she was doing
when she moved that insipid *always* due east.
That the region of the heart is impenetrable ever,
that knowing the beast doesn't shame him,
that proximity invites peril, that even
with his snout smeared in huckleberry juice,
his eyes too tiny to detect you in the bramble,
he is the intimate who stumbles toward you,
navigating by smell alone, with damage in mind.

adversaria

It is a vivid anecdotal detail (but no more)
that the earliest item of Roget's personal belonging
coincides in its ideational substance with his last
and most successful work. They were surprised to find
massive palindromes—hairpin-like structures
that contain DNA sequences that read the same
backward and forward. Are we not drawn onward
to a new Era? The system is robust,
and it doesn't depend on the weather.

ON THE PHOTOGRAPHS OF EMMA BEE BERNSTEIN
(1985–2008)

Trying to see a face detached from its life among the senses
is like trying to understand the angle of a bone without
a view of the musculature that animates it. Are we aware
when we command the gaze of our children,
that beyond the stone circle of here and now, the code
they are likely to copy into their neurons will feature
frames of strangers, cartoons, cameos of fancy
and horror written side by side, so one draws up the other
like a drowned pet from the depths of a well?
And how will we know when the unseeing begins,
when the family begging at the exit becomes a tableau
of figures in a mist, or the distended belly of the starving child
lapses into apples and oranges of light and shadow?
It's not enough to pass on distrust of forms
or to point at one's own blindness saying
don't as I do, especially don't as I. And
the long disordering of the senses Rimbaud
claims for art is a madness children already know
like the remarkable Emma Bee gone at 23.

LOST PHOTOGRAPH OF MURIEL RUKEYSER

Both the original and the copy are gone,
she to signs. And that which we called *portrait,*
brought out of the red dark of my first husband's
basement photo lab with its purpling edges,
is thirty years buried in the insufficiency
we call *memory.* In the room where he took
what we innocently called *pictures*
were witnesses, I among them, then wife
to the eye at the lens, who lived to tell,
though some of those present in the rapture
of the great poet's *presence,* are now also dead,
and some of these have left their own wake, *texts*
we'd have to say now, though we still adored
the hierarchy of genre in those days.
Because Fred in his signature trench coat,
black notebook open in his left palm,
familiar profile fronted by thick glasses
was bent to the task of capture. Where is it now
that famous notebook, familiar to the point
of sacredness to a handful of students
then in training for an *ars* that was already
busy disappearing and would achieve it
by the time we arrived where Fred was,
propped against a radiator in an overwarm
visitor's apartment of a small college
in the Midwest. The Sage whose choice bits
the now-dead teacher chose to keep was so close
to her own heartstop she couldn't walk that day
across the quad from dorm to classroom. Within

the year, she'd be a fodder of what had been
said by and about her, and whatever Fred took
down in that notebook—map, double, mirror—
maybe not at all what we were scribbling there
in the ignorant confines of memory,
a capture of gems humming from the fragile
old woman, but Fred's own doubts, doodles,
epithets or lists. All I know is I was there,
twenty, and reverent with belief in Fred
who appeared to believe in Muriel,
all of us there by virtue of luck, chance,
and another dead woman's gift of funds,
and maybe I wasn't even married yet
but intending to be, the man
behind the lens all potential still,
taking and taking and taking the shots.

"The psyche emerges from the most complex
corporeal structures."

—François Dagognet

The huddle of spine swaddled in dirty tee shirt
and arched into serious study is a five-year-old boy
squatting over his Valentine box
trembling with concentration as he deigns,
just this once, to use the battery of pinks.
He's worn his cache of blues to nubs,
and eliminated purples from his palette too.
But greens suffice, and reds do not offend.
He wears his colors overnight, painting
his pillow like a warrior Celt
as he conjures claws and heft, a taste
for the big and the mean. Here is the workshop
wherein we learn at last what's in that wallop
of genes. Wielding cutlery pistols and sticks
before he shed his baby fat, now poking
is the way he knows and loves a thing
no matter what the script of dents and knots
undoes. Before the sparkly hearts are dry,
he's piled all the sofa pillows into fort
and fired his sweet vestigial tail
against the heap. All fodder, fur and fury,
he's bound to roll the sturdy carcass
of imperative against even this,
his glittering box for tokens of the heart.

NOTES ON A SUPRASTERNAL NOTCH

What you've fallen for is part and gap
in the pectoral girdle, bone that rotates
along its axis like a key turning
in a lock. A skeleton key,
a lock with a hole so dark
it appears to have no teeth.

Little key that could be turning
here on the rungs of the abducted
shoulder even as it is also that other
sweet key of the groin pressed
into service by as little as a view

of a man squatting to reach
for a towel on a summer beach,
his shoulders forward so the stunning V
of him ignites in your own nether notch,

a touch of what made you and makes you
new, signature of the first ossification
the body knew, as well as the last
to collect its cargo of minerals
into a matrix of bone.

adversaria

Boys who were hoarse had cloves and gum arabic given them,
and a delicate boy was supplied with a "pocket pistol" containing port wine,
which he swallowed just before his solos. The ears, boneless
and the only part of the head not integral in its structure,
are apt to be regarded, by brutish people in authority,
as easily removed appendages. Unless introspection deceives me,
I believe that when I visit a zoo my muscular response changes as I move
from the hippopotamus house to the cage of the weasels.

CAMBIATA

The male treble voice achieves its maximum power and resonance just as it is disappearing.

—Andy Martin

It hardly matters now whether we loved the child
because he was real or because he was not.
He played the boy soprano who charmed
his way out of a wilderness of lack, his clear
voice risen like the surprise of a slender moon
finding its way between racks of cloud
and pouring its whole into the visible wick.
But what's left of Jean-Baptiste Maunier
is only this moment held in the membrane
through which we will always have to pour
a beam of borrowed light to see again
the pale boy with the eyes of a wolf
drop his jaw and sail the cadenza
note by note from the rampart rim
before he's smothered in a sheaf of whispers
on the street, *frimousse, chérubin, ange.*
The life we remember him living
was never his own, and the voice too
he'd have to render back unto the fiction,
that gift of unseen gods whose punishment
is simply that the man will have to wear
the clean surplice of his child self
perpetually, that he will be handed
the microphone again and again

by some fallen star in a circus
of TV light, and deliver ever after
only ordinary music, the round nub
of his Adam's apple rocking in grief.

ATTIC

The eaves are ears that funnel blast and squeal
from the road below, shouts on the water,
cutlery dropping on the stone patio
of *Au Paradis,* where an Arab wedding
goes all night, and the man stretched
to sleep beneath the eaves across the street
breathes to this music, accepts its thrum
along the places where his muscles touch
the mattress touching the frame, touching
the floor, touching the beam, the stone wall
that drops to the cobble touching the road
against the wall across the street under the feet
of the dancers, themselves collecting throb
from the stone on stone on stone. The man
alone in his bed is there with them
dancing at another wedding, that of his childhood
friend at a restaurant in the south, the village
of their youth tucked into mountains
that carried their own rumble into boys' bones,
one that would hum in ribbons of asphalt
for thirty years before they came home men
and clapped each other's shoulders
where the root of wing still reports
its percussive throb. He needs to sleep
but he doesn't want the noise of it
quiet yet, its weather of possibility,
promise of coupling, conception,
a connection that is not pure idea, not
the flimsy melody of memory,

but the body with its thoughts
shaken out like a rug, his skin
and bones clean instruments
with which all possible horrors
can be driven from our midst.

COLETTE AS TROPE

Why should we have to know the difference
between ourselves and our constructs, a pure
thirst and its first unholy register? In the shadow
of the body's grim teleological march,
who cannot admit to a voyeur's eye
languishing along the boy's clenched fists
of unripened muscle? Who has not bent
for what spoils at a touch, the trail of apricots
and lilies that can train a boy to wait, to turn
against himself, to go without?

Autant-Lara's 1953 film of *Le Blé en herbe*
opens on children singing at the seaside
until a storm stomps in and upends umbrellas,
sends nannies scurrying to scoop their charges
toward dark interiors, while Philippe, rowing
on the sea, is overturned and washed up, naked
on a beach of school girls roped together
at the waist by their mortified supervisors
who drag them away as the naked boy
emerges from the sea. White, slippery
and narrow as a skinned fish, Philippe
lies face down in the sand, the boy of him
figuratively dead. When he comes to
and looks down at his nakedness

beneath the film's frame, we all know
he cannot go home this way,
so he crawls toward the cliffs,
plucks up a straw beribboned hat
the roped and tittering girls have left
and holds the thin moon of it
across his newly offensive crotch.

There is no more story beyond this one,
the boy overturned by the storm of the woman
in white, potent and cruel in her advancing age
and the storm of the girl who loves him,
potent and cruel in her lavish youth.

He already knows his body has a plan
and his mind will have to lend it
something resembling reason.

adversaria

        The effect of fetal decapitation on testicular descent
was studied in the pig. Gubernacular development was unaffected
and testicular descent occurred normally in decapitated fetuses.
European colonists of the Americas and the Pacific took with them
all of their genes, but contributed almost none of their mitochondrial
(maternal) DNA to the local populations; in contrast, they spread
a generous number of their Y chromosomes. So many dynamos!
The only possible conclusion is that oxytocin is an altruistic hormone.

ECORCHÉS REDUX

After seven on a weeknight it's all ladies
at Snap, but the pictures of tiny flayed
men riding recumbent cycles and pressing abs
keep us company, swagger in our heads
like the seven dwarves swarming our resolve
for better butts come May. They pump
their red packages in racked brochures,
in plastic placards by the door, admonish us
to wear the beepers after hours
in case our knees buckle into ash,
or our hearts skid with clog.
The mirror forces everyone to watch
her own fierce visage, beet stain soaking
the row of cheeks until we all match the fat,
red valentine bulging in its glass box,
ready to shock us back to life. Like it or not,
the flayed toy soldiers prance through
our hypnotic submission to the body's iron
resolve to reduce itself to lean meat,
and in the dizzy swirl of endorphin high
all of us allow the subconscious film
to filter up through the fluorescent lights,
the dream of a serious, precise and much
bemuscled man not flailing but flying
through the long strands of our collective ache.

BIDET

The body's oldest lace, tiny knotting
of sensation around love made in a stairwell
in the city of violets, buttons for light at each
turn that gave just enough current to ignite
half each flight at a time—as if someone
understood there'd need to be ropes of darkness
flung for the tongues to catch.
River of stairs, pouring up and up, the room
somewhere above, a dull approximation
of a grand plan hatched long before we were forged
in fire like this ourselves. Flame pinched
from a candle pocketed before we stumbled
through the swath of velvet drapes into wind
from the sea. This was a man
who moved around my body with urgency
and care in one motion, who would not love
and yet would not do less for the body
open to him. I would never understand
and never not want that attentiveness to my mortal
flesh again. Spoiled for the acolytes of our own
time and place, we return in the wane
of want to this gasp in the planet's clumsy
yearning, where men make love like gulls
riding the ordinary gift of wind, and women
give up the face of God between their legs
out of a holiness so old even the smallest inns
provide a bowl in which it may be washed
clean every time.

ROGET'S

There were years when she hid it, the yellow sheaf
with its broken spine cloaked in masking tape,
or the fact that she needed its spurious lists
branching into each other like the fragile
twigwork on a climbing rose. It held *sky*
away from *sty, clove* from *cleave.*
Who knew that the architect himself needed
to cheat, found the unbreakable syllables
rolling away like so many marbles
spilled from a child's palm? She depended
on this approximate taxonomy, which turned out
to be code following invisible instructions to rise
through a canopy of hardier species.

Very like, one of the stranger ways of saying yes.
From Old English *lich,* body or shape, likeness,
a bodily sensation of similarity and the notion
that we warm for what repeats us, favor
that familiar we could feel with our fingers in the dark,
the round of cup on the desk, or a knob finding the palm
exactly where it should be. Rendering most similar to,
as if the visage too were map of wishing, blue eye
seeking blue, and ruddy cheek seeking more
of its own rudiment. Yes, then, to the face as synonym,
a seeking after echo, ultra, extra, a plus us.

The doctor rounds the curve of the outer ear
on the desk, *your ear* he says, though it's anyone's
crude appendage, the fragile curl of cochlea behind,

the stem of Eustachian below and blocked
with a tiny row of ovals that could be canoes or seeds
gathering under the starburst of infection.
We could take the pencil from his spotted hand
and finish out the sketch: all the cranial tunnels
he has missed pressed under the sockets of the eyes,
how the interior unfurls: cochlea, drum, incus, malleus,
stapes, ampullae, membranous labyrinth, vestibular
nerve, auricularis superior. Are these tunnels
and chambers not gorgeous in their reach, echo
of an aria the snail scooting its soft curl inward
will perform in the empty gallery of the skull.

adversaria

If the boy is undergoing a growth spurt with a noticeable height gain,
his larynx and its associated skeletal and muscular anatomy
will be undergoing similar enlargement. . . in a normal healthy boy
it is an unstoppable process. If a piece of the baby's lung sinks
when thrown into water, so the theory goes, it proves
that the child never experienced respiration,
that it was stillborn.

PHRASED BY WOLVES

For as long as I can remember, the phrase *my mother*
has arrived in the gap between thought and speech
when I'm tired, trying too hard to make party chat
where the narratives spin, each from some burr
or knot on the one before, and we finger the mist
on the bottoms of our drinks as if the next way in
were written there. *My mother*—I know better
than to actually utter it, realize its role as place
keeper, cognitive stutter, cosmic comma. It's not
the sonic hum of it that matters, or what semantic
underthings it might dangle in the room.
It's a door rocking open without agency,
a place where the wall of consciousness breaks
into blankness, and not, as we might expect
subconsciousness, though that is where speech
would go if thought did not snatch it back.
My mother never fits the talk at hand,
the spirals and eddies of mildly remarkable news,
so when the phrase rolls toward the precipice
of my tongue—*my mother my mother my mother*—
I can still kill it, knowing perfectly well
that if it gets loose, the others will turn to me
surprised, their own *mother* contexts spinning
for a fit, and finding none, raise
a wall of eyebrows. Someday, however,
the tenacious phrase will simply gush, *my mother,*
my mother, like some warm and shocking
bodily fluid over the tongue's worn threshold,
will hitch itself to a sentence that has nothing

to do with she who bore me, will reveal itself as mere
reflex of mind akin to the knee's uncanny release
at the tap of the doctor's mallet, so the question is not
why *my mother* comes unbidden to the door,
but what will happen when she doesn't knock.

WHEN MENTHOL WAS QUEEN

No blue beckons so much as chlorine blue,
bottom of the pool blue, faintly bearing the faces
of flushed mothers, astringent partner to rubber loungers
welded to the backs of the knees in seconds.

We of the inland summers crave only this blue,
this gorgeous replica doubled and rocking
beneath even a fierce sky. Now we know
what they were doing when they raced away

in their hot bucket seats, our mothers, craving
a smoke on the patio, the long coil of phone cord
caught in a screen door. Fuchsia Jell-O and orange shag
nothing to the long gash of turquoise

to which they delivered us. And thirty years
before we even wondered where they went or why.
The satisfaction of an entire knotty-pine kitchen
scrubbed in Liquid Gold only lasts so long,

and cans of pillow mint green meant to cover
every inch of the garage yield up only enough
bright toxin for a season, beyond which we
of the bar codes, box stores, and breast pumps

are expected to proceed differently. And do,
though the arrow will eventually find us too,
bring us back to the blue wedge from which
we can finally see her huddled in the cove

between spruces out back where her smoke rises
into the cool prickle and pucker, delivering her
from each fierce escape she can imagine,
all her fancy, hanker, and aim in blue dissolve.

VESTIGIAL

He arrives at rivalry, though it wears
the name of the man who owns the shirt.
He claims he smells his way from trace
to name, but act and react fuse
into an impulse I cannot follow
being woman and becalmed
by that same scent that riles the boy.

Logic will not read this power
nor even associative thought,
though idea and chemical fire
spring up along the budded synapses
like pairs of hydra heads in every space
left open by the breaks.

The child believes he can divine
cures for predicaments of fact,
absence, for example, still in the realm
of the mutable, denizen of the mind's
open pools where fears rear, then plunge
into the fins and webs of the known,
and joys ride the body's minimal expanse

of flesh, all sensation leading up
to a smile's flush across a visage
that still fits in a parent's open hand.
Who wouldn't want to freeze him

here in the forest of magical foray
where scent itself is knowledge, not cause,
and the mind's brutal appetite for dichotomy
has not yet shot from the depths.

adversaria

*The Y looks like a purple pansy in the NIH diagram; in the Wellcome,
like a red glow worm. Elsewhere, pink and fuzzed as a pair of kissing
slippers. Nowhere does it appear sleek, muscular, or even a cool blue.
It stands aloof and haploid, and, for most of its length, fastidiously avoids
the messy business of recombination. The eyes above the nose and mouth
keep the vision above the shadow cast by the body. Matisse, for one,
confessed to having lusted after the naiveté of children's art.*

SECURE MATH

He's supposed to draw each coin,
but the quarter is a square "Q"
the dime a triangle, the nickel a capital "N."

Either somebody is experimenting with icons,
or there's an explicit desire to blur image,
text and symbol so the child
will never guess their separateness.
Understands and uses estimation.

Only the parent instructions, elaborate and tedious,
reveal when words are wanted, when numbers.
How many broken circles does it take to make change?

The child thinks it natural that the mother's new beau
would like to meet the father's mother.
Predicts and describes probability.

The teacher shows the parents two new ways
to play war with an ordinary deck of cards.
Kids love these, she says, ignoring the father's quip
that poker offers more complex skills.

The father finds this curriculum inane,
but he's found a way to add his mother, son, second wife,
and her new man to a room without him.
Renames, compares and orders numbers.

The child is supposed to locate a food item on sale this week
and draw the coins that match its cost, but he picks
the free eggs and skips the second step.

Where, in the child's flesh will these reckonings lodge?
Little hotels bathed in quaint pastel neon,
or rebar towers? Sirens going by them all with equal speed.

He's supposed to cut out triangles with numbers
in each corner and recombine them endlessly.
Practical skills are emphasized in this curriculum.

Long before he saw his mother's beau,
he smelled coefficients in the pillows,
found Euros in the bottom of her purse.
Understands place value.

Satisfied, it seems, with new equations,
he unlocks his plastic pig, lines up his stash
from collective pockets, jars, and car trays,
the leavings of our least significant
transactions repurposed into assets.

His teacher collects the year back into its blue
binder, taps it twice like a magic door. *Secure
math,* she assures us, is just that, what it's safe
to assume he knows.

CHILD ASLEEP IN A BASS CASE

He will not wake for Brahms
or Elgar, but wind in the minarets
is magic, and the low hum
of trucks arriving to stock the bar
with honey cakes and wine
sings in his spine. Temerity
too has a voice in the blood
that sweeps in from the Istanbul
night. Eardrums are actually
cheek-bone ascended as we left
the water. This velvet is meant
to spare the instrument damage
in transit, red any way you brush it,
soft if your shoulders are burnished
wood, but a wrath
if you are made of flesh.

adversaria

The famous Dr. Buck of Norwich would take a piece of tissue paper,
the size of a postage stamp, hang it by a fine thread in front of the mouth,
and make the boy sing to it without blowing it away. Gifted to Caroline,
Princess of Wales, Peter never acquired any interest in sex,
did not laugh, could not converse, but hummed all kinds of tunes he heard,
loved onions, brandy and a good fire. Despite the passage of children
in and out of it, childhood, as a social space, remains.

DIARY OF A SENTENCE

Don't we all begin with what is on the eye?
So that I, *Sentence,* am place, wonderland,
torture chamber, boudoir, closet,
whatever can be locked behind a door:
blue key, gray matter, *skeletons*
that open anything.

Nothing to do with that once dubbed *soul,*
like a film in the wrong language,
heart, genius, and the sweetened *fancy*
layered and colorful as a *petit four.*

What stops the momentum? Late hour
in the life that winds a spotted hand
around the pen? Such an old-fashioned
notion, *the pen as penis,* that easy bleed
from one *petit mot* to the next, obsolete.

So have screen and key effectively
neutered me: where once we said
put pen to paper do we now say
fingertips to keys? Well then,
every and any sex can play.

We say *deep in the heart of winter,*
yes, I've worn that lacy garter,
but where did winter get a *heart.*

The business is to stopper the ears
for the long sail through
all that screaming
to find (oh, whisper it only) *song.*

But some poor souls are unlucky
enough to have a dram of memory.
Soul was gone before we were born,
but *heart* lingered in hard places
like winter or tree trunks,
and even, once, in stones,
story, still lifes, self, shh . . .

So it's a matter of wrapping around
the forbidden part a copse of other contexts,
con + texts, bad texts, convicted texts,
the happy legions of negation. As if there were
such a thing as a *protext.* Protest not
my love, words will ever desert us:
rapture, sublimity, ardor—underworld words,
the tips of the fingers now so entirely adept,
they are one with the eye moving across the snowy
document, inside the bonny bone of the head.

CHOIR SCHOOL

In the bleak light always shed in church
basements, I watch the girl's father
manage a meal for sixty choristers.
He hovers above a triad of steaming pots
and broadcasts to the few thin women setting tables
just how cheap the meat really was.
His daughter offers a white cake trimmed
in yellow hearts, while the teacher's single hummed
note unspools a song of thanks from sixty throats.
Every voice teacher the daughter has ever had
has advised her to lie down after a meal,
though she doesn't know precisely why
the being prone is vital. Some trick of the body,
thin strands of blood filling with clean
breath, so the meal can make its way
into and through the child like a necessary sequence
of notes. And the parents welcome the mystery of this
with faraway smiles. O cake and song go down as one,
lighting up some screen in the nourished brain—
yes, this very basement with its banners and arks,
linoleum and blonde doors open again
on barrels of paper plates and plastic forks
wadded into the end of a familiar repast
and stored against uncertain futures
while the noisy flight of choristers
disappears up the stairs to their own
century, a swarm of sated neurons.

RELINQUISHING THE FUSIONAL MOMENT

The first sign is his rejection
of the French lullabies. The second,
a predilection for meat,
three, standing up to pee. Next
I expect, he'll nix the armada
of furred species arrayed in tubs
around his room, the turtle knobs,
hippo chair, and everything Pooh.

I'm becoming another planet fast,
a hurtling ball of foreign gases
visible only on the darkest of nights.
So it's no surprise that when I take
someone else's infant in my arms,
the moist skull delivering scent
of cellared apple and worms,
I know the garden gate is already
locked, and we are in the bloody
woods.

TWO-PART SONG FOR LENT

> *He was with the wild animals, and angels attended him.*
> —Mark 1:13

> *When at night I go to sleep, Fourteen angels watch*
> *do keep.*
> —Humperdinck's opera, *Hansel and Gretel*, II.2
> libretto by his sister, Adelheid Wette

Perhaps they were never at odds, the beasts
and angels in the proverbial wilderness.
Certainly my child finds them twinned,
squirrel, lion and angel all apart from what
the world offers to his touch, and yet
he knows the lion's heart is sometimes
good. He sighs at cartoon tiger moms
who bathe their young with tongues,
believes in hippo dads who waddle
and fling their feces as they go.
He knows what hunger is.
I'm the one who's troubled by the myth
of perspicuity in stories, the fact
that this concert hall of children under ten
is witnessing two parental figures
scold and send their hungry children
into darkness, admonishing them to stay
until they've filled their baskets. Or that
the dangers in Mark's version of the forty days
are far too inexact: Satan's out there, yes,

but the beasts are only wild, the angels
merely tending. I'm supposed to guide
the child in moral matters, and yet I'm partial
to the singing witch in ruffled bloomers,
cannot confiscate the elegant Babar
or cavalier cat in boots who torments
peasants into treason. Nor do I yearn
for the day when the beloved cub
who's refused for twenty pages to take
his bath, becomes a wild beast again.
I glory in the feral prayer, spilled milk,
the story of parents at the end of all reserves.
The little elephant's dapper spats and weakness
for Haussmann style elevators are every bit as gospel
as the fourteen angels Adelheid invents
to keep her children safe
from what they cannot help but love.

adversaria

Most animals come in two readily distinguishable forms.
Always ephemeral and insufficient, meaning inevitably
requires something more, something in the body itself
and, at the same time, beyond it. This is what enables us
to go on living. Boys who survive stress in the womb
live longer on average than those born during steadier times.
When speech is energized through the principle of the sigh,
we have singing.

LOVE NOTE

ce petit message glissé sur l'oreiller

This little message slipped under the ear's
soft province, to which cheek, crown,
every aspect of the human head inclines,

sails its lispy ballet of secret
under the busy village of the inner
ear, where a child is about to tune

a bright violin to the consummate ting
of a fork. Regrettably, it's only idiom
upon idiom, a pirouette of phrase quaint

only to the un-French; nevertheless, apple
and rose, part sustenance, part charm.
Once having caught it is commotion enough

to unspool all manner of extravagance,
like the amaryllis we coddle in its tin tub
all winter, the flaking, loamy knob

already trying its translucent spikes,
one of which may unfurl into a parasol so heavy
it must be staked over the sad bananas—

while the child and I recount the marvel
of the stalk's waxy progress, not the bloom,
but the story of the bloom, which is so

inexorably orange finally, we forget
what we were expecting all the long
green going, now that the light has left

the single window that poured sun
on the shortest day of the year,
its whole reason for being there at all.

GIRL SLEEPING ON A TRAMPOLINE

Summer finally plays out
like the colossal blue ball that sailed
shadow over the fence in a fine
rain of squeals, where neighbor girls
freighted a circle of springs with sighs
before their parents packed them off
to lakes and norths where they'll nap
safely adrift in dragonflies and lily knots.
But this one stayed behind,
alone in a house peopled the year
with siblings and bickering. She wanted
her August fabulous with evenings,
cars floating on hormonal bloom
from one basement rumpus to the next,
imported gins and triple sec ferreted
in sips from fathers' stashes,
each burning bottle's neck polished
with the heel of an alarmingly
capable hand, until this morning
finds her on the lawn, crush of hungry boy
still turning somewhere down there,
so she climbs into the still trampoline,
covers her eyes with hair that no longer
smells like her own, and aims one round hip
at the clouds, glad to have arrived
nowhere near the earth.

VERITABLE NUN

Sweeping in from the blasting sunlight in white robes,
she's the very picture of divine emissary, surprisingly
nimble in all that yardage, young, even pretty,
and I realize I haven't seen a nun that young
since I was a child. I hold the door for her
as if God herself has arrived in the Department
of English at last. The robes are heavy as canvas sails,
surely hot, full as they are with folds of shadow
and the thrash of her inside them as she moves,
but it's only later that I think of the body. For the moment
of her entering, it's her face that turns directly to mine,
smiling, a radiance so frozen it seems to come
from a far and gothic place where nuns
were that mysterious portion of someone else's
church, and as apt to fly as to pray. Both souvenir
and history, her face floats free of human markers,
ear and neck and rampant fall of hair
all pinched in their starched frame, so what's left
moves its severed muscles in palpable grace.

When she's gone, I want only the puff of air
on my bare legs that her robes gave passing,
the smell of dough. Yes, she was alive,
and that expression, gleeful, impish,
promising some kinetic tomboy frame beneath
all the high gliding, what she's had to hide
to keep, sturdy calves that put her, miraculously,
in my way again as I drive home, though now
she's about to take flight in the hot yank

of summer wind. She turns like a girl before a triple mirror
trying to see herself from behind, trying to count
how many of her selves escape, before the eye
returns to the first one, God all over her face,
tipped into the sun as she waits for the cross light
to change.

CRANIAL LANDMARKS

Perhaps she never had anything resembling a reason
for the way she stared at his angular jaw, the shine riding its curve,
the throb of his Adam's apple a finger's breadth below.
Something in her rose on tiptoe to get a better view
even while thinking herself invisible, though "thinking"
hardly describes a nine-year-old girl's first marking
of a male secondary sex characteristic, the sudden knowledge
that this boy has swallowed something forbidden and works it
just below the surface where mockery and temptation
lie together like the thieves they will become.

He's only three years older and nothing new since he's always lived
two doors down, but this is the first time she's been squarely next
to him, the bright welt of the patrol belt casting a glow
along that jaw, the heavy wooden pole held parallel with the curb
on which she now balances, its shredded flag stamped
with the giant octagon-enclosed warning. Half a century from now,
the part of her brain that draws a finger along this particular curve
will have added the mandible of a young German
riding the S-Bahn from *Wannsee* to *Charlottenburg,*
a boomerang of bone that disappears in every stroke of sunlight
and returns with such force she knows it will mark what it hits.

adversaria

The brain itself, is, in origin and development, only a sort of great clot of genital fluid held in suspense or reserve. As wines age in their barrels, part of the wine evaporates (known as "the angel's share"). All of the vital mechanisms, however varied they may be, have always one goal, to maintain the uniformity of the conditions of life in the internal environment. The stability of the internal environment is the condition of the free and independent life. Rumours of the Y's demise have been greatly exaggerated.

SNOW ANGELS

When he comes to,
runnels of guilt dried
down the drained globes
on the mantel and the fire cold,
he will not know
who committed the act,
though his own hands
ache with the memory
of cudgel and something borne.
Only then will the faces
of his children rise up
out of his palms
on the heads of nails,
bright ideas of mercy,
which also pours now
from what others call "heart"—
old skeptic, that dream
you only have once.
Now what to do with the woman
here, still asleep in unfortunate
belief. It was his body after all
given for hers, the price
of which is a great arc,
cold angels of this
flapped into the ground of her,
gift and gift and gift.

THE AGE OF REASON

Seven, they say, and here it is, fear
of death arriving right on schedule
with note-reading, math and the last
of the milk teeth. But whoever dubbed
this stage "reason" must surely have
been given to jest, fear being reason's
most ironic twist. More absurd still
is the fact that it strikes the child
as he sits, naked and slippery, on the pot,
so I have to clean him up before the hugs,
the trotting out of hideous clichés.
Clouds and beards and miracles,
"mystery" suddenly a word I'm glad
to own. *Will I get to keep my head,*
he wonders, *and what about my clothes?*

I saw her, though, he says, *lying in the box,*
the neighbor lady he watched for signs
of life until the popsicles stopped
coming through the fence, and hoards
of people he'd never seen arrived to cull
her things. Giant orange plastic Monarchs
nailed to the garage, even her thermometer
so large we could read it from every room,
disappeared from the garden, signs
that neither temperature nor life
were guaranteed to last.

Each scenario I offer lasts a week at best.
First, the possibility of magic, then science,
a potion he could toss from outer space
to keep us all intact, including lions,
maybe grandmas too. What he understood
without my help: that most adults would be
unwilling subjects, so he'd have to fly by night,
salt us back to life with stealth.
But a college boy at camp brought down
the mothership by telling him
it wouldn't work, he'd have to die.

Finally, there isn't any other word
for why the old lady's head
didn't go to heaven with her. I have to
trot it out; skeptic that I am, it hurts
to hear it leaking from my mouth, "soul,"
and worse, to point at my own heart,
sweeping out and up to fit the body
to the air, to own the only story I know
that quiets the terrible noise
of reason headed for planet earth.

THE STILL-FACE PARADIGM

We speak of that which has no face by what it lacks.
What looks back is visage, vista, precipice
on which we see ourselves in ersatz tableau.
For some, the empty cowl falls back,
and the void gazes out with requisite contempt.
For others, a mask raises its plaster moon
from the depths of slack-jawed sleep, lucky
and smooth. But scooped from a bin in the vault,
the face of a severed head is scored with panic,
gray as a garden slug and hard, a windfall apple
blistered with frost, writ all over with literal
out of the blue. Done with mirrors,
this ridiculous grimace says each feature
has read and understood its own worth at last.

PHARAOH

Hot wind like the breath of some animal
hopped up on the conviction of its own
prowess. The sweet spot of summer
snuffed in a spit of rain, and now, the child
will absolutely not take off the braided thread
someone has wound on his creamy neck. Badge
of his first week on his own in the woods,
badge of his bond with boys I do not know,
games and plates of meat and spiders
I do not know, the charge of ruddy teens
clacking away on hormones and cleverness.
He appears suddenly in the clearing
in someone else's shoes, hauling his suitcase
full of woods, wet socks, something
faintly metallic, and I understand that
in no time at all, the world knit up
the welt around my exodus, made way
for a new order. This one seems benign enough
with its pranks and contests, loon counts
and the tiny gold moons of the thumb index
by which he found his way to the old stories
and the new word blooming on his tongue
pharaoh. Somewhere behind his voice now
are things that belong to him alone,
predawns in a kayak, the cold rope
of a snake against his wrist, scent
of his tribe tumbled from sleep,
a sugar of sand rubbed from the edges
of it all, in warm little stacks at their feet.

adversaria

One evening he got lost in the Rue d'Enfer and his governess could not find him until after dark. It was only after sniffing at her hands and arms two or three times that he made up his mind to follow her. Law, be it religious or secular, emerges as the key mechanism that mediates between, but also preserves, the boundaries between adulthood and childhood. The Armenian mole vole, for example, has diverged into two species, one of which survives without a Y or SRY.

INCHWORM

Such a trouble, Desire. Hers, freighted
with disconsolate wish and waft of firsts,
frog, dark puddings, Endust, years ago clover,
wet clutch of the church nursery, and the fat
scallops of wool carpets dragging their burn
behind her elbows, mother cool and orthodox
as dining-room wainscoting. Then His,
bike oil stripes, garage metals and must,
gold seams of strap sweat, brother's strange
creaminess, and the shining vinyl
of the sisters' stack of 45's warming under
needle drag, gauze of their leaked eggs,
father's hard blue, and mother's need clapped
like bare legs around them all.

Finally this Child in the viscous light
of summer seed drift, hot boy breath
closing in on the tiny worm arcing green
in the palm of the girl who found it. He
watching her watch the arc and inch,
arc and inch. So he'll want tomorrow
to try with his own spine and upending,
to know not only the worm, but the hand
of the girl and what it was like to be
in it ever and enter, to mash, wear and eat,
to inhabit, unravel, inhibit and so delicately,
very greenly and fragrantly unlimit.

DESCENT WITH MODIFICATION

The other side of deep is a kettle of different fish
brimming away, the sky after which they seek
a pail of notness, not him, not us, not the usual paste
of past. In this one we remember what we said
and old monkeys bloom in the tween,
but these are not paws we use often,
so who knows how efficient they'll be
in another cup, the other side of deep.

We won't want to go where we are
tonight, a dish of snails curled in the butter
of about-to-be-born-again in Café L'Express;
Paris has crawled onto land summarily delighted
with feet, and though we know more French
than we did in the drink, the other side might be Farsi,
might be yellow, might be right, but won't be
here, our wish in the eye
of storms and ruined shoes.

There is a city our marsupials never tippled,
those puppets from a novel of manners,
and the lilt of the marble beneath our elbows
tells a better story about knees
than we were expecting. Outside the cabs
swim down Park like an army of beetles
lifted from their sure little toes,
and wine drains away somewhere below
to a facsimile of hell we can certainly smell

but which we'll evade with the usual shower
of illogical choices until we come to the other
side, where there might be fire or batons of light.

There is no way to keep the souvenirs of fin
or feather claimed in the street. It's only
on the other side that we realize
there was more to be nibbled from the mullion
of familiar, backed, as we were, against wet wall
by a weight we were always and still
going to swim from but not quickly
nor with perfect resolve, because the girl
got left on a whorl loving the scales,
bones and pockets of gone-again, frozen
in hello's fine "o," with its acrid after
brine of *tant pis* while the marvelous spears
of new old lady iris keep poking the scrim of her air.

That proverbial kiss is, however, the rather
and sweeter that lives on the side of deep
we have to leave to live. Nothing love about it.
Squamata tiptoe behind, kyas out of the sea,
and still it isn't for them to name what's so far down
no one with a neural swirl can survive
the descent. More importantly, it's not true
that he turned and lost her forever.
Green kumquats knot above them
so they don't even think to desire,

and neither is it true that she reached for
nor discovered anyone naked, let alone buck.
They never left the soup at all,
but sleep entered their skin like divers,
and words were risible bubble and ooze
because there were only ever the two
of them until the other side arrived
like a truck from the city and fired
its world of cargo into the crowd.
Not all mutations matter.

So no, we can't remember what it was to drown.
In the street where the cab never stops,
rain marries soot in our shoes
while the much-anticipated kiss
hardens into Art, and the other side
wakes as a fiction unspooled in our palms
directing us to go on inside, sit down,
and read the veins of wine stitching bouquets
into the white napkins cast in our laps,
all phylogenies arriving at that about-time spine
that is, after all, buried alive.

adversaria

One cannot promise fertility for any male child, and the undescended
testis—no matter how it is managed surgically—is less likely to be fertile.
No, it never propagates if I set a gap or prevention. Although modernism's
utilization of the "other" traditions has often been remarked on and
analyzed, its utilization of the pediatric other has not. "No human face
could stand having 30 death masks made from it," Gruppioni said.

LUNCH IN THE TUILERIES

Kneeling in the dust with a good stick
and the hard nose of baguette purloined
from our meal, he crushes the bread
onto the wand, and props it in a chair.

When the fearless pigeons of Paris dive
for his offering, he runs at them, arms open,
teeth bared with a brutal glee even the waiters
dodging rebuffed birds find cute.

How is our laughter at this good?
The shade is full of parked strollers,
precious cargo of new flesh fattening
toward the same instinctual goal.

What power there is, children claim like a sweet,
a desire not grounded in need, but arriving
nonetheless in their consciousness,
an itch to rule even this makeshift roost. The birds

don't learn, but the child does. And if we were to say
such terror is *terrible?* To affect that measured
parental voice that divvies up the world
in rights and wrongs while also imparting the sense

that it's all completely provisional? This moment,
unchecked, could rip a lifelong seam
through the child's still-soft neural tissue,
a gulch of yesness that can't be filled except

with more terror. Because there *is* a future
in which he'll build a trap for something larger,
fly at it with this same face on which glee's gone
savage. All I know is: were you to appear

in the garden at this moment as threat
to that boy body scooped from my own,
I too would wear such a face,
and I'd be aiming to kill.

THE MISSING

They who would not make the national news
were their loss less gruesome in detail,
the artificial leg chucked behind the barn,
the "unspecified amount" of blood
that in its very mystery blooms a blue
contusion in the mind's unwitting hospitality
to treachery's suburban tracts. We will not admit
to collecting them, but someone does.
Their open spaces long for strings of code
we could execute with scripts we know,
each harrowing an invitation to a crime
we dream our own, dream from which we wake
radiant with guilt, before the cogs of possibility
revert to useless zippers in our skin.
Then we understand again that our minds
might not, after all, be our own to close.
The missing live inside a slim chance
like that, an act as dreamed as done.
Were we awake at the reported hour,
or merely lost in task, departed from chronology
in hot pursuit of some compelling counterpoint?
The toddler on the beach transfixed by some
bright enticement making for the sea,
the girl so busy naming imaginary babies
she's failed to draw the weapon of her key.
In the tiny hammer of that unguarded moment
both are suddenly flush against the world
they left, and though their familiars keen

for them, the rest of us, such perfect strangers,
watch the tiny banners of code add up
and hope to learn exactly what it was we did
and whether or not we ought to run.

FAR FROM THE FLOWER

De Formato foetu, 1631
Pregnant female figure in vivo, anterior view

She's open from the navel out, petals
etched with veins and tapered into points
that float the child on billows and tiers,
like a gift to a king or a ring to a bride,
trailing the unruly tendril of his cord
while mother leans one beefy knee against a tree,
so a branch can leaf itself between her thighs,
and hide the brutish corridor of love.
Her oddly flat and mannish breasts are shoved
above the meaty rose, and aside from flying coif,
no one could ever guess these strapping thighs
belong to any body bound to bloom.

FAUNA

Some mornings she sits in the boy's room
after he's gone and feels she's guarding
something, perhaps from the roofers
next door who carelessly drop their nails
in the grass, perhaps from the growl
of the saw down the alley, a man
assembling a fence, another clanging apart
a motorcycle, or the roar up of the Comcast
truck, the stucco contractors horking chew
at the curb, the pissed-off recycling guy
tossing down one more page of rules
about what does and does not go.

The roofers crawl across the roof hip,
hammering steadily against the morning
birdsong, their butts jammed up in the sun
like giant babies sleeping on their arms,
and she realizes that she has always observed
men sideways, the smell of them spelling
a long habit of fear even now that she's become
invisible; further that she's mistaken the boy
for flora, prized perennial coaxed from spring
to spring, her mind absently collecting
the dates of first furl, first bud, as the roots
inch almost imperceptibly south, escaping
the massive maple's voluminous shade.

What the child has chosen to save,
to feature on the dresser's tidy archive

is a mystifying collection of candy
he will not eat, a trio of metal pigs,
the baptismal bowl heaped with thumb-sized
fighters from myths she does not know.
There was never a time when she knew
what the boy was thinking, and today
she's sure she never will, though she's learned
to close her eyes and breathe his stink
back into the dark inkling she was born with,
to ride the fluent reflection on his retina: white
moth lost in a smear of dogwood flower;
the cottonwood drifts, a trove of clouds
brought down by seeds so small, most
will never root. The bright clot
of an earthworm chopped in half
to learn how much it can lose
and still survive.

adversaria

    *When a boy is left with a single functioning testis we recommend
anchoring it to minimize chances of losing it to torsion later in life.
"Revenge" is found under "Retrospective Sympathetic Affections"
as the antonym of "Forgivness." The palindromes are not just "junk"
DNA. Of the 12-13 cranial nerves that affect cerebral function,
five are at work when we kiss.*

LEMON

You will only know me the way the ribs
of a lemon know the sky, which is to say,
not at all until I'm opened.

You will know me as an alphabet of spiders
adding up to whatever your own prior
experience of spiders can tell you.

As the embrace of your arms crossed
around your core in the sleep of those
who've lost the husk of the espoused.

As the back of the bright rind
where sugar rounds the curve
and branches into bitter cure.

As the roof of the closed mouth,
the underside of a palm where the veins
defy the crease's bright future.

It is the way of all desire not
to manifest as a body whose familiar
odor rises from the sheets no matter

how many times they've tossed
in the hot O of the dryer, tiny spots
of our uncapped selves printed there

like the stars they were when first
we accepted them as light.

THE BODY APOLOGIZES FOR ALMOST EVERYTHING

For overriding your good sense,
for tormenting you with hungers,
addictions, fevers and pox,
for my failure to flood at the touch
of one who could have made you
happier, for the lateness of the hour
in which I finally gave up
the egg, for the contractions (hardly
God's punishments but my own
prodigious inventions, meant
to let you know who would always
be in charge), for the ligaments
I sprang apart, for the stone I wedged
in your breast, for the arches
I collapsed and the spine I bent
like a hanger, for the spasms
to remind you that luck and fate
have nothing on me, for the hard edges
you translated into the mind's silly dream
of supremacy, for the bright welts of itch
I raised each spring of your childhood,
for the burning of the milk against
the rips I opened under the child's
first teeth to bare the seethe beneath,
for the bones I am whittling to air
now, the nails that flake like shale,
for the roil in your blood at the sound
of a laugh on another continent,
for the storms of heat drenching

your pillow, for the fine lattice
I etch over the backs of your hands.
Above all, for casting you in the way
of so many who desired me
while you were mere afterthought,
for the consequent howl of heart,
the course of havoc I've wreaked
when you couldn't get me close enough
to what I made you want, then need.
What did I care that they would disappoint?
I had what I required, and you, my girl,
I made you free.

THE ART OF HUMAN BALLISTICS

The Human Cannon is the last spectacle on offer
this Saturday early in the toddlers' final year
of toddling, and the cheap seats put them so far
from the ground that the tiny manic terriers

racing toward the elephants seem no more
than insects zipping toward an opportunity to feed.
These mothers would certainly have said no
to the Shriners, had they not succumbed

to the glamour of "circus," the very word
a star burning in their own unperturbed pasts.
Though now they look at each other over
the children's heads, sure of the mistake.

One mother makes the usual inquiry,
everything, after all, in the guise of lesson,
Your favorite? And the beaming boys
do not have to think to find the thrill,

The shooting! Oh, says the mother.
Though she's already pedaling back
through milder possibilities, hoping
to repair the unfortunate attraction

and the strange taste of guilt in her mouth.
Why not the elephants lifting their slippered
feet with the care of the very old, or even
the pastel poodles lurching along in tutus?

But there is nothing left of the afternoon
except the one they call The Human Cannon,
the oblong bead of red launched in a sneeze
of smoke and boom the children believe

is man as actual ammunition, unfurled ball
of flesh blasted toward the unlikely heaven
of a circus dome. Of course they think it's hot
in the dark cylinder of the gun, that the blast

is surely lethal to anyone but him, prelude
to all the stalwart immortals they'll seek
in years to come, but for now shooting and flying
are still married to the marvel of human volition,

flight by fire, spring or compression
of air, something they do not guess that life
will actually offer them in increments
as acrid as the powder still wafting in the air.

adversaria

    Why did little Hans not decide to fear telephones, or automobiles,
or heights, or bugs? The more "natural" the standard of delicacy and shame
appears to adults and the more the civilized restraint of instinctual urges
is taken for granted, the more incomprehensible it becomes to adults
that children do not have this delicacy and shame by "nature."
We lived in a bell that rang all day. The syllable may have evolved
as a by-product of the alternate raising (consonant) and lowering (vowel)
of the mandible, a behavior already well-established
for chewing, sucking and licking.

BEES

Yes, worry the word hard, the phrase, the color,
the semantic family's breaks and fissures,
know that every bride to thought is doomed
to less than hope demanded. Not the Word,
only one letter short of All, but the little one
that wore its bravado even in utero, from a time
less in love with future as a cause, when utterance
was barely dressed and smelled of grass,
when there were fewer paths behind,
or so it seemed to a girl with one thin shelf
of books, none of them leading backward yet,
down sturdy canonical cobble that had brought us
so far we forgot there was ever a way.
Through enormous catalogues of toils, lost
to a reliable grunt and root against the rich mire
of surface. Lost registers of local fish and rodents,
tools, vehicles and skiffs, a quantity of sunlights,
meadows, myths, weapons, kinds of wound,
lost before we ever got them to the tongue's
small unfastening of a sound we'll never learn
to hear. Like a girl, wild for the right silence,
who clamps the fiddle under her chin,
and fills her jaw with bees, countless,
precise, every one a perfect possibility
turning in its airy grave.

FACE NOTES

It's easy to forget that this is no longer
an image bathed from emulsions, let alone
the promised concentration of sense organs,

hairline tiptoeing away from the brow
in imperceptible increment precisely so
we could read the features

and, like any practical piece of architecture,
the windows well above the body's shadow
and protrusion. Perhaps we close our eyes

and seek the oldest part of the human face
to swallow its uterine song, wander the soft vale
of the philtrum, and remember a time

when the nose was not so much obstruction
to our pleasure, but tipped so the mouth
was more bud than seam, the whole cranium

more mass than moraine. As we never learn all
of a word at once, so too we take the face
one context at a time until the mind

lays down a geometry at once familiar
and mobile, but what we draw from the wet welts
under cover of darkness is not in any realm

the mind makes. Rather, it dwells in trace,
before the face raised its monument of bone,
when the mouth was one note

not yet shushed from song.

Terroir

The mind's easy essay into anger turns, suddenly,
and runs along the bank of wild grape burgeoning
over the fence, more dense this year than ever,
dropped like the virgin's voluminous blue robes
as if from a great height to cover some poor angular shoulders
hunched into a cradle for her child. That fence
gives onto the good neighbors, while the one between us
and the bad ones wears no robe of vines, and rots continuously
in any weather. The children on the other side of it
alternately call out variations on bodily emissions
and threaten to kill all passersby. Nothing I've planted
covers the bare view through to their garish purple house,
nor muffles the dumb thwack of their father's fist meeting
flesh, the mother's holy Shop-Vac fired up against the screams.

The earliest named boy singer was the young David, whom we may infer was about 14 years of age when he played the lyre to calm King Saul (1 Samuel 16:23). He was old enough to travel alone but not to fight. The presence of hairy ears has often been described as the only Y-specific trait. God saw I was dog. If asked to point to the "you" in one's head, most people indicate a place just above the bridge of their noses.

TRIGGER-HAPPY

Orange, orange, orange, and impossible to know
which says *hunter,* says *don't shoot,* says *November*
has robbed us of color. Therefore bright fleece vestments,
caps that cast the glow of health down into the children's
snowy cheeks. The boy and the girl go out fluorescent
against the sky's wicked blue, raise toys and sticks
into horizons along which they sight. She strikes
a girl detective pose, eyes aligned along the bat
she aims at me. He concentrates, perfecting
his Elmer Fuddish grimace for mommy's ready lens.
We're all shooting with our own ratchet of joy. They'll kill us
with cuteness while we kill them with slippage,
allowing, for once, the little insurgencies of marshmallows
in lunch's stead, sleeping in bags, peeing on trees.
We thrill to each rule we break. The children lead us on
into the dawn's unholy volley of shots, each a possible carcass
we might get to see roped to a roof tomorrow afternoon,
each a fleeting doe the mind will pepper with a little
trigger itch. After cocktails on the deck, we'll mommy-smile
while old Looney Tunes slide above the children's toes
encased in fuzzy bunnies and sleeping bears.
An old man shoots the crafty magpies because he cannot sleep,
and though they pop up feather-bald in mock outrage, they win
and win again. At dark we watch another story of talking totems,
wolves who learn lessons meant for children,
how to venture ice and peril toward a storied self.
The mother tells her daughter, don't *you* do that,
but by now the children know we're guilty
of inconsistent threats. Packing out on Sunday,

we know we'll get a show on the road,
trailer after trailer of steaming carcasses in piles
of tangled angles we'd never see in life. Even the shiny
pair of hooves that juts above a pickup's rim
counts. And we are counting them, counting ourselves
in the game that began in exuberant orange and aim.
Because we saw the pleasure the boy and girl made
of costumes we meant to protect them, we said yes
to so much we thought we were against. In the pretense
of shooting back, we were caught in the crossfire
of the pleasure of more pleasure, the spectacle
of children's faces lit with the cruelty of the novel,
and now we are all hurrying home to dress the meat,
cooling the comestible flesh under pine boughs,
bright plastic tarps and tales, closing the window
on magpies who could not die,
traffic at a standstill for hours while we count
trucks, racks, toes, and yes, we say yes to everything.

ALL ABOUT SKIN

On a reasonably sized female adult,
two square yards of the stuff,
all etched with nerves wild
to be roused, altogether the largest
organ in the body. Unless you count
the considerable accumulation
of disappointment that sprouts
as fast as creeper in a chemical-free
yard. Or all those useless tears,
salt and mucus and plain old water
manufactured by the ducts every time
hurt shows up for dinner, rather more
often too, as the years advance,
putting his feet on the sofa,
leaving dishes in the sink. Perpetually
twenty with his tight ass and gorgeous
hands, he invents longing like a tall tale
and gets us to drink one more glass
of merlot than we'd meant to tonight.
If only we had more feathers and horn,
that sweet jacket of wooly lanugo we wore
in the womb and swallowed like a marvelous secret
just days before the world turned on the lights
and pronounced us girls.

Petite poupée sur commande

Ne convient pas aux enfants.

45 euros gets you a doll of him or her
you love, though in the interests of art,
the face she makes is always only half—
one eye mid-wink, a mouth skewed left,
a beard scrawled sideways over where
an ear should bloom. On their backs
it's also possible to order up a message,
a little alphabet of pricks and stitches
to detail your command: *désolée,
je t'aime, va te faire voir.* The dolls
are hardly lifelike, though that's not
the point; they carry your keys or adorn
your purse. Like giant squid washed up
on shore, the larger models sport
limbs that dangle, arms not much
distinguished from the legs. These ballerinas
know that going limp convincingly
requires work. In fact, even their skin
is in the realm of costume: a dainty print
of posies, grids, and doodles spirals up the calf
to meet a calculated flounce above the knee.
Or perhaps you'll want the open button
at the neck's imaginary notch
where, if you love, you'll want to sneak
your tongue. For a little more, the artist
will even make the whole into a scarf,
a wearable beloved, sweetest mockery

at a price you can afford,
appearing first as clean affection,
even tribute, gesture to lay claim,
yet ready also, quite conveniently,
to reverse its role, become the doll
you'll need to rend with pins
because it looks too like a thing
that, after all, you cannot use.

OBLATION

In the dank hole of the locker room,
I unbuckle the straps from under his skates,
lift the hard globe from his head,
and slip the dripping wedge from his teeth.

Trying hard to be supportive of this sport,
I snap a picture of his moist curls fresh
from the cave of the helmet, cheeks
stippled with risen blood, eyes flashing

with blue exertion. But a man across
the locker room stops me. No pictures
allowed. By which I suddenly understand
that someone could be here for illicit thrill,

boys ripe with sweat, packing sodden gear
in bags they cannot lift without adults.
I think of my boy's bliss at owning
his first nut cup, and how it isn't me

he wants to help him unlace the skates
but his father, or failing that, any
of the dozen burly strangers milling
in the hall. I've given my only son

to this company of men who crave
the white and unforgiving oval of the rink,
who grunt and dive for the chance to add
their mayhem to the fray. They all adore

the rush to punch a cuneiform of dents
against the boards, the spray of shards
that blasts from the blade's bright veer
and flies in the caged face of the foe.

adversaria

Sex hormones are mostly made of grease while peptide hormones
are made of meat. Ovaries are soft tissues; they leave no fossils behind.
If there were a word for love other than "love," says the doctor
who worked with her first, it would be that I felt for her. The capacity
for receiving ludicrous ideas appears to be completely denied to animals.
Add somewhat to the length of the Snub, and give it a turn upward,
and you have the Celestial nose—le nez retroussé. "Science bodies
think this is art, and art bodies think this is science," he said with a laugh.

BOY AT THE CENTER, INTERVENING WORLD

Dinosaurs gather on his tie, and he turns
whole profile self violin blondeness again
turns, dinosaurs staying put toward the lens
fierce little violin under and pointing
increments of left with looking, looking again
cheek smeared gold—oat slime? God's thumb?—
cheek going after the profile and gaze going
off also left to what might have been face
voice stranger or toy not caught except
in some neuron the result of which
worms in for use in some remote
moment turning toward what looms:
equal enemy wife parent not even body
turning just this angle violin going
first toward not even ear simple hope
in light not ultimately this but turning
a profile like this and larger with new
neurons glinting off of this peculiar
particular simply because we caught it,
we own it. We have it down.

GIRL WITH A DUCK IN HER LAP

In a few years, someone will use this picture
to justify his disappearance from her life.

It will be the way she bends her elbow to contain
the jut of the duck's breast, its suggestion

of the way she might hold a sleeping child
across her knees, form a cradle that frees

and captures all at once. Or it will be
the perceived sangfroid on the duck's face,

the bird's unwitting cozy-up to human flesh
that frightens the boy who's old enough to father

and young enough to spurn it. Already in love
with the fountain of his own seed, he likes

the idea of peopling the world with a wave
of his various selves, but the weight of this bird

in a lap where his own temple has sometimes
found the providence of fit, fires something loud

against the far walls of the mind's unfurnished cavern.
Then there's instinct's famous tendency to enter

in Elizabethan dress, replete with rapier
and tights, that ruched collar of noble birth

all too like a newly feathered nest,
so the only question left is whether or not

the boy can tell the girl with a duck
in her lap what it is that fetters him with dread.

THE WONDERS OF WEB CAMS

Though I've never laid eyes on her actual skin,
I've combed her pixelated smile like a surgeon
in search of the body's random wrongs
and found her again yesterday in line
at the cosmetic counter, certain it was she
though I've never seen an image of her
from the back, never been close enough
to smell what unraveled our lives
like a wad of yarn between the instinct tutored
paws of a cat. Even the shape of her skull
is a patent unknown, always softened
by the long hank drawn over her right shoulder
again and again in the little fire of my screen.

Each year when the light arcs north
and the stubble breaks out in stubborn greens
I'm cast again into the whorls I learned
as my fingers found the faces of her there were
to find. But the voice did not endure,
girlish, irritated, swimming in captured stills
and sealed like old letters in my soft tissues
with the dangerous toys and secret longings
of a childhood too remote to conjure.
All that's left is the little whine of her denial.
The heart registers terror well enough,
so we locate love in its lumpish
constancy, while the mind goes on
inventing impossible wheels, the round
and round of the human face, this inexorable

patch of familiar features that belongs
to a woman who chose not to look back
at one who still sees cartoons of her
hoisting her generous breasts to the tiny eye
at the top of the screen, so they can ride
the impulses out of her Boston townhouse,
bounce from tower to tower across
a country of oblivious sisters, and arrive
in time for breakfast at the address
I once called home.

THE FORBIDDEN EXPERIMENT

Someone has lovingly wrapped
the bowl of a discarded toilet
in black plastic and left it for months
in the alley. Even shrouded,
the neighborhood boys know
its true identity and dream of how
to sneak a pee. The throne has begun
to list like a ship aground in current,
rocked alike by alley residents
gunning away from irritation,
spat, and odious task, or simply
coming home in a violet dusk,
wondering what imagined offense
the plastic intends to prevent.
That Nature might reclaim it?
That some creature seek its hard
throat as providential haven?
Or that some wild-to-mar graffitist
discover its porcelain skin?
Were it not for the rapt attention
of my child who marks each episode
in the pot's alley sojourn
(how it receives rain, falling leaves,
the bank of dirty snow shoved
from the plow's dutiful blade),
and improvises on its wide array
of potential fates, I myself
might never have noticed it
squatting in the weeds.

adversaria

Drinking water at the window, Victor appears to swallow
the light in the bowl. Thirst is actually an emotion
which can be triggered by panic because it is hormonally controlled.
If it's true that mostly our fears define us, then no, he cannot return.
Two colors are equiluminant to an observer if switching them very rapidly
produces the least impression of flickering. A liar can reproduce
the feeling that a wilderness does.

Souvenir

Remember is not a reflexive verb in English,
like *perjure*. To remember is not to *remind*,
though it is to welcome into the mind
a veritable lived moment that has embossed

itself in some durable way. For new love
we bring scenes swept into maudlin corners,
and we love that the lover *pays* attention
(it is no accident that attention is to love

what cash is to commerce) to what the rest
of the world might call narcissistic or worse.
If I told you my mother practiced smoke rings
on the patio while my sister and I were safely shut

in neighbors' rumpus rooms, you might find
your own mother suddenly on a porch, in a car,
in the grove beyond the fence with that same cigarette
and yourself flushed with some golden thing at the thought.

Though what the mind chose to save is variation
on a theme, barnacle drawing detritus into a carapace
built on someone else's narrative. Whether you count it
narcissistic depends on how much mystery

or misery you can weld to the terraced substrate
of a childhood. Memories are a coin of the realm,
as good for sales, science and industry as for love.
Let's not forget that hell has circles too.

A NOTE ON THE ADVERSARIA

Pronunciation: /ædvər'sɛriə/

n. Properly plural, but in English usage often a collective singular. A commonplace-book, a place in which to note things as they occur; collections of miscellaneous remarks or observations, = miscellanea n.; also commentaries or notes on a text or writing. *Oxford English Dictionary*

The adversaria are not footnotes, end notes, or explanatory notes. In fact, they are almost all collaged direct quotes from sources listed at the back of the book and represent the poet's attempt to leave a trail of breadcrumbs from her forays into disciplines beyond her own in search of answers to questions the poems themselves collectively ask and only provisionally answer.

The direct quotes preserve discipline-specific rhetoric and the aspects of "voice" these linguistic habits produce, and isolate peculiar but compelling "facts" delivered by real or self-described experts. The adversaria set these discipline-specific voices against each other, as well as against the poems themselves—and remind us that "information" is (often delightfully) unstable and always at the mercy of its own rhetoric.

ACKNOWLEDGMENTS

Grateful acknowledgment is made to the following publications in which these poems first appeared.

American Literary Review, "Roget's," "Colette as Trope"
The Antioch Review and *Poetry Daily*, "Y"
Cerise Press, "Attic," "Two-Part Song for Lent"
Great River Review, "The Lucifer Effect," "Vestigial," *"Terroir,"*
    "Veritable Nun," "When Menthol Was Queen," "Fauna"
Harvard Review, "Ecorchés Redux"
The Huffington Post, "The Missing"
The Literary Review, "Balcony over Rue de la Huchette,"
    "Child Asleep in a Bass Case," "Relinquishing the Fusional
    Moment," "Boy at the Center, Intervening World"
The Lumberyard, "Far from the Flower"
New Letters, "Diary of a Sentence"
New Ohio Review, "All about Skin"
Ninth Letter, "Descent with Modification," "Love Note"
Northwest Review, "Bees," "Inchworm"
North American Review, *"Petite poupée sur commande"*
Notre Dame Review, "Face Notes," "Lost Photograph of
    Muriel Rukeyser"
Prairie Schooner, "The Wonders of Web Cams," "Trigger-Happy,"
    "The Body Apologizes for Almost Everything"
Quarterly West, "Phrased by Wolves," "Bidet"
River Styx, "fizzee óllэjee"
St. Thomas Magazine and *Caper Literary Journal*, "Hyperphagia"
Southern Humanities Review, "The Age of Reason"
Southern Indiana Review, "Girl Asleep on a Trampoline,"
    "Snow Angels," "Choir School"
Verse Daily, "Love Note"

REFERENCES

Angier, Natalie. *Woman: An Intimate Geography.* New York: Anchor Books, 1999. Print.

Autant-Lara, Claude, dir. *Le Blé en herbe.* Franco-London Films. 1953. Videocassette.

Baker, Mary. "Wine 101: Disgusting Things in Wine." E-Gullet Forums. *Society for Culinary Arts and Letters.* October 26, 2004. Web. <http://forums.egullet.org/index.php?/topic/54275-wine-101-disgusting-things-in-wine/>

Barratier, Christophe, dir. *Les Choristes.* Perf. Jean-Baptiste Maunier. Pathè. 2004. DVD.

Beet, Stephen. "Boy Sopranos and the Lost Bel Canto Tradition: Extracts from a Paper Given to the Guild of Musicians and Singers at All Hallows by the Tower, London." *The Better Land.* November 2005. Web. <http://www.thebetterland.org/bland052.html>

Benzaquén, A. S. *Encounters with Wild Children: Temptation and Disappointment in the Study of Human Nature.* Montreal: McGill-Queens University Press, 2006. Print.

Bernard, Claude. *Lectures on the Phenomena of Life Common to Animals and Plants.* Hebbel E. Hoff, Roger Guillemin, Lucienne Guillemin (Trans.). Volume I. Springfield, Illinois: Charles C. Thomas, 1978. Print.

Bernstein, Emma Bee (1985–2008). M/E/A/N/I/N/G Online. Susan Bee and Mira Schor, eds. Web. http://writing.upenn.edu/pepc/meaning/Bernstein/

Billock, V. A. & Tscou, B. H. "Seeing Forbidden Colors." *Scientific American.* February 2010: 72–77. Print.

Bloom, Paul. *How Children Learn the Meaning of Words: Learning, Development and Conceptual Change.* Cambridge: MIT Press, 2002. Print.

Bragg, George. "An Approach to Vocal Technique." *The Big Book.* Boychoir, Past, Present and Future. December 6, 2005. Web. http://www.boychoirs.org/library/education/vocal002.html

Brophy, John. *The Human Face.* New York: Prentice Hall, 1946. Print.

Candland, Douglas. K. *Feral Children and Clever Animals: Reflections on Human Nature.* Oxford: Oxford University Press, 1993. Print.

Colenbrander, B., van Straaten, H.W.M. & Wensing, C. J. G.

"Gonadotrophic Hormones and Testicular Descent." *Systems Biology in Reproductive Medicine.* 2 Jan 1978:131-137. Print.

Cooksey, J.M. "The Male Adolescent Changing Voice: Some New Perspectives." In M. Runfola (Ed.). *Research Symposium on the Male Adolescent Voice.* 1984: 4–59. Buffalo: State University of New York Press. Print.

Dalke, Kate. "Sex and 'The Y.'" Genome News Network. June 27, 2003. Web. http://www.genomenewsnetwork.org/articles/06_03/y_chrom.shtml

Darnton, Robert. *The Great Cat Massacre and Other Episodes in French Cultural History.* New York: Basic Books, 1984. Print.

Dormann, Geneviève. *Colette: A Passion for Life.* New York: Abbeville Press, 1985. Print.

Dubuis-Grieder, C., Schöni-Affolter, F. & Strauch, E. "Differentiation of the Gonads." *Human Embryology.* Swiss Virtual Campus, Universities of Fribourg, Lausanne and Bern. June 27, 2007. Web. http://www.embryology.ch/anglais/ugenital/diffmorpho02.html

Elias, Norbert. *The Civilizing Process: The History of Manners.* Oxford: Wiley Blackwell, 1939. Print.

Gelbart, Nina. *The King's Midwife: A History and Mystery of Madame du Coudray.* Berkeley: University of California Press, 1998. Print.

Gombrich, E. H. "The Mask and the Face: The Perception of Physiognomic Likeness in Life and Art." In Gombrich, Hochberg & Black, (eds.) *Art, Perception and Reality.* Baltimore: Johns Hopkins University Press, 1972. Print.

Howe, Fanny. "Bewilderment." *The Wedding Dress.* Berkeley: University of California Press, 2003. Print.

Hüllen, Werner. *A History of Roget's Thesaurus: Origins, Development, and Design.* Oxford: Oxford University Press, 2004. Print.

James, Alison & James, Adrian. "Childhood: Toward a Theory of Continuity and Change." *The ANNALS of the American Academy of Political and Social Science.* May 2001: 25–37. Print.

Jobling, Mark. "Lands of our Fathers: Y-chromosome Diversity and the Histories of Human Populations." *The Human Genome.* Wellcome Trust. June 24, 2003. Web. http://genome.wellcome.ac.uk/doc_wtd020875.html

Jones, Ian. "X and Y Chromosomes: Sex and Death." *The Human Genome.* Wellcome Trust. October 9, 2003. Web. http://genome.wellcome.ac.uk/doc_WTD020741.html

Kemp, Sandra. *Future Face: Image, Identity, Innovation.* London: Profile Books, 2004. Print.

Kendall, Joshua. *The Man Who Made Lists: Love, Death, Madness, and the Creation of* Roget's Thesaurus. New York: Putnam, 2008. Print.

Lane, Harlan. *The Wild Boy of Aveyron.* Cambridge: Harvard, 1976. Print.

MacNeilage, Rogers, & Vallortigara. "Evolutionary Origins of Your Left and Right Brain." *Scientific American.* 24 June 2009. Print.

Martin, Andy. "Choral Divisions." *The Times London.* 20 December 1997. Web.

McNeill, Dan. *The Face: A Natural History.* Boston: Little Brown and Company, 1998. Print.

Meyer, Barbara. "Sex and Death: Too Much of a Good Thing." The Meaning of Sex: Genes and Gender. *Howard Hughes Medical Institute Holiday Lectures on Science.* 2001. Web. <http://www.hhmi.org/biointeractive/gender/>

Newton, Giles. "The 'Maleness' Chromosome." *The Human Genome.* Wellcome Trust. October 9, 2003. Web. <http://genome.wellcome.ac.uk/doc_wtd020746.html>

Newton, Michael. *Savage Girls and Wild Boys: A History of Feral Children.* New York: Picador, 2002. Print.

Nosek, Leopold. "Body and Infinite: Notes for a Theory of Genitality." 46th IPA Congress for Psychoanalytic Practice: Convergences and Divergences. Chicago. *International Psychoanalysis.* July 2009. Web.

Odent, Michael. "Preventing Violence or Developing the Capacity to Love: Which Perspective? Which Investment?" *The Association for Prenatal and Perinatal Psychology and Health.* Winter 1994. Web. http://www.birthpsychology.com/violence/odent1.html

Page, David C. "Sexual Evolution: From X to Y." *The Meaning of Sex: Genes and Gender. Howard Hughes Medical Institute Holiday Lectures on Science.* 2001. Web. http://www.hhmi.org/biointeractive/gender/

Pound, Ezra. "Translator's Postscript" to Remy de Gourmont, *The Natural Philosophy of Love.* New York: Boni and Liveright, 1922. Print.

Pullella, Phillip. "Dante Gets Posthumous Nose Job." *Reuters.* 12 January 2007. Web.

Putnam, Hilary. "The Meaning of 'Meaning,'" *Mind, Language, and Reality: Philosophical Papers.* Cambridge: Cambridge University Press, 1975. Print.

Quintana-Murci, Lluís & Fellous Marc. "The Human Y Chromosome:

The Biological Role of a 'Functional Wasteland.'" *Journal of Biomedicine and Biotechnology.* 2001:18–24. Print.

Riding, Alan. "Hypothesis: The Artist Does See Things Differently." *New York Times Magazine.* 4 May 1999. Web.

Rutter, Michael. *Genes and Behavior: Nature-Nurture Interplay Explained.* Oxford: Blackwell, 2006. Print.

Shattuck, Roger. *The Forbidden Experiment: The Story of the Wild Boy of Aveyron.* New York: Farrar, Straus and Giroux, 1980. Print.

Skaletsky, Helen & Tomoko Kuroda-Kawaguchi. "The Male-Specific Region of the Human Y Chromosome Is a Mosaic of Discrete Sequence Classes." *Nature.* 19 Jun 2003: 825–37. Print.

Svoboda, Elizabeth. "Manly Science: The Latest Findings on the Curious Y Chromosome." *Popular Science.* June 2006. Print.

Symes, Colin. "The Adulteration of the Infant Aesthetic: Modern Art through the Eyes of the Child, *Journal of Aesthetic Education.* Autumn, 1996: 107–110. Print.

Truffaut, François, dir. *L'Enfant Sauvage.* United Artists. 1970. DVD.

University of Michigan Health System. "Testicular Descent." Health Topics A-Z. n.d. Web. http://www.med.umich.edu/1libr/urology/testicular_descent.htm

Walter, Chip. "Affairs of the Lips: Why We Kiss," *Scientific American.* 12 February 2008. Print.

Wells, Samuel Roberts. *New Physiognomy, or, Signs of Character, as Manifested through Temperament and External Forms, and Especially in "The Human Face Divine."* New York: Fowler and Wells, 1894. Print.

Whitehead Institute for Biomedical Research. "Y Chromosome Sequence Unveiled." *The Human Genome.* Wellcome Trust. June 18, 2003. Web. http://genome.wellcome.ac.uk/doc_WTD020714.html

LESLIE ADRIENNE MILLER'S previous collections include *The Resurrection Trade, Eat Quite Everything You See, Yesterday Had a Man in It, Ungodliness* and *Staying Up for Love.* She has been the recipient of the Loft McKnight Award of Distinction, two Minnesota State Arts Board Fellowships in Poetry, a National Endowment for the Arts Fellowship in Poetry, the PEN Southwest Discovery Award, two Writers-at-Work Fellowships, a Pushcart Prize, the Billee Murray Denny Award in Poetry, and a number of prizes from literary magazines, including the Anne Stanford Poetry Prize, the Strousse Award from *Prairie Schooner,* and the *Nebraska Review* Poetry Award. She has also held residencies and fellowships with foundations in Switzerland, Spain, Germany, Scotland, France, and Indonesia. Professor of English at the University of St. Thomas in St. Paul, Minnesota, since 1991, she holds degrees in creative writing and English from Stephens College, the University of Missouri, the Iowa Writers Workshop, and the University of Houston.

Book design by Kim R. Doughty. Composition by BookMobile Design & Digital Publisher Services, Minneapolis, Minnesota. Manufactured by Versa Press on acid-free 30 percent postconsumer wastepaper.